This book of miracles belongs to:

_____

_____

_____

STRENGTHEN YOUR FAITH THROUGH JOURNALING.

Faith journaling, or Bible journaling, is a way of exploring your faith creatively. You can write or draw, use art supplies or office supplies, write in a Bible or a notebook…whatever feels right for your journey. The prompts in this book can help you get started. By taking the time to sit down and engage with them, you'll feel more connected to God. So set aside some time for yourself and your journal, and turn the page. May it be a valuable step on your faith journey.

*"The moment I connected my faith
to my creativity, everything changed."*

—Shanna Noel—

creator of Illustrated Faith
(*www.illustratedfaith.com*)

Everything came into being
through the Word,
and without the Word
nothing came into being.

John 1:3

Your word is
a lamp before my feet
and a light for my journey.

Psalm 119:105

Think about all the people you encounter in your life—
your family, your coworkers, even the people you smile at on the bus
or make small talk with at the grocery store.
What are you grateful for about them?

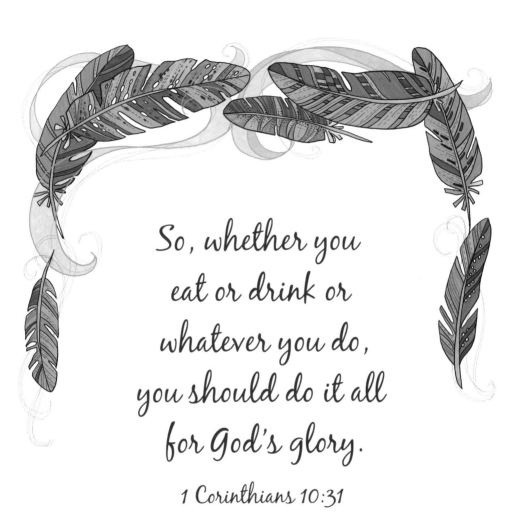

So, whether you
eat or drink or
whatever you do,
you should do it all
for God's glory.

1 Corinthians 10:31

When you picture a miracle, you may picture water turning to wine. But sometimes miracles are in the smallest details—a leaf budding or a baby learning to walk—and they can happen every day. Look closely for everyday miracles today. What do you find?

Don't you know that
you are God's temple
and God's Spirit
lives in you?

1 Corinthians 3:16

All who believe in me
should drink!
As the scriptures said
concerning me,
"Rivers of living water will
flow out from within him."

John 7:38

Nature always wears the colors of the spirit.

Ralph Waldo Emerson

Some people experience God in a place of worship, in the outdoors, or in the home. Some experience God surrounded by others; some when alone. Do you have a place you like to go when you need to get in touch with God? Where are you, usually, when you feel closest to the divine?

I assure you that
whoever doesn't
welcome God's kingdom
like a child
will never enter it.

Mark 10:15

The next time it rains, try to find a moment to really listen to it. We tend to rush through rain, worrying about driving home and frustrated by its inconvenience. But it, too, demonstrates God's majesty. How does it make you feel to listen to the rain?

_____

_____

_____

_____

_____

_____

_____

_____

_____

_____

_____

_____

_____

_____

_____

_____

_____

_____

_____

There is **beauty** surrounding us in the simplest of things

Don't neglect to open up
your homes to guests,
because by doing this
some have been hosts to
angels without knowing it.

Hebrews 13:2

If I have such
complete faith that
I can move mountains
but I don't have love,
I'm nothing.

1 Corinthians 13:2

Be
JOYFUL
in hope,
PATIENT
in affliction,
FAITHFUL
in prayer.

ROMANS 12:12

42

You may live with, work with, laugh with, and/or travel beside many of the same people every day. You support them, in large or small ways, as they support you. How are they doing on their journeys? Who could use your prayers?

Be tolerant with each
other and, if someone
has a complaint against
anyone, forgive each other.
As the Lord forgave you,
so also forgive each other.

Colossians 3:13

The idea of a "home" has so many meanings. Perhaps it's a building; perhaps it's a feeling; perhaps it's something else. What does it mean to you? Where do you truly consider your home?

We give thanks to you, God
Yes, we give thanks!
Your name is near.
Your marvelous deeds
are declared.

Psalm 75:1

LORD, you have done
so many things!
You made them all so wisely!
The earth is full
of your creations!

Psalm 104:24

Nature
is
splendid
beyond
compare.

As you experience the beauty of nature, whether in a mountain or a tree root, you may find yourself reflecting on the majesty of God surrounding you. Have you ever felt that way? Describe a time you felt God's presence in nature.

Heaven is declaring
God's glory;
the sky is proclaiming
his handiwork.

Psalm 19:1

It can be difficult not to get frustrated with the stresses of daily life.
As you go through your day, think about what tends to
stress you out. Perhaps it's an opportunity for reflection—
how can you find God in your stress?

He will cover you with his *feathers* and under his WINGS you will find *Refuge*

PSALM 91:4

Don't be anxious about
anything; rather, bring up
all of your requests to God
in your prayers and petitions,
along with giving thanks.

Philippians 4:6

Don't you know that
your body is a temple
of the Holy Spirit
who is in you?

1 Corinthians 6:19

It can be hard to honor our bodies regularly. We're constantly confronted with messages about beauty products or potential health problems. But your body is with you every day, and, after all, it's a temple of the Holy Spirit. What are you grateful for about it?

Come to me, all you who are struggling hard and carrying heavy loads, and I will give you rest.

Matthew 11:28

We fill our lives with art, from museum-quality oil paintings to our children's crayon drawings, from simple patterns that make us happy to music that touches our souls. What are you drawn to? Have you ever felt God's presence in a piece of art?

_____

_____

_____

_____

_____

_____

_____

_____

_____

_____

_____

_____

_____

_____

_____

_____

_____

He has made everything beautiful in its time.

Ecclesiastes 3:11

From his fullness
we have all received
grace upon grace.

John 1:16

Don't fear, because I am with you;
don't be afraid, for I am your God.
I will strengthen you, I will surely
help you; I will hold you with
my righteous strong hand.

Isaiah 41:10

There is one spectacle grander than the sea, that is the sky; there is one spectacle grander than the sky, that is the interior of the SOUL.

Victor Hugo

Think about the things you have done in your life—the easy and the difficult, the happy and the sad, the fun and the frustrating. What are you grateful to have experienced? Why?

What the Lord requires
from you: to do justice,
embrace faithful love,
and walk humbly
with your God.

Micah 6:8

Think about your community, whatever that means to you. Perhaps it's your neighbors, your child's school, your place of worship, your city or town, your country, or even the group of people you talk to online, even if they aren't close together physically. What about your community are you thankful for?
How could it use your help and prayers?

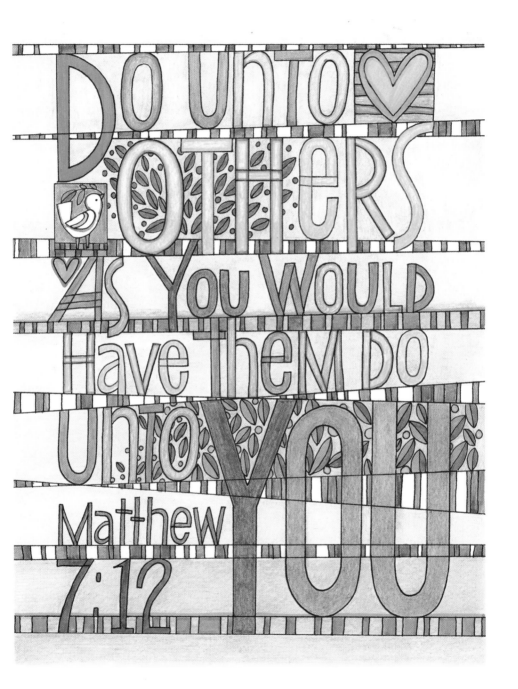

Those who dwell
on the far edges
stand in awe of your acts.
You make the gateways
of morning and evening
sing for joy.

Psalm 65:8

My God will meet
your every need
out of his riches
in the glory
that is found
in Christ Jesus.

Philippians 4:19

It's easy to be self-deprecating when you get a compliment—it's easy to downplay it, volley it back like a tennis ball, or ignore it. But what if the compliment is a sincere expression of gratitude? Really listen the next time someone compliments you.

Let the connection happen, and be sincere in your thanks. What is the experience like?

Even when I walk
through the darkest
valley, I fear no danger
because you are with
me. Your rod and your
staff—they protect me.

Psalm 23:4

You dwell in your home every day, so it's all too easy to take for granted what God has given you. Spend some time, as you move around your home accomplishing your everyday tasks, thinking about and appreciating it. What are you grateful for about it?

AS FOR ME AND MY HOUSE, WE WILL SERVE the LORD.

JOSHUA 24:15

Peace I leave with you.
My peace I give you.

John 14:27

117

The earth's depths are in his
hands; the mountain heights
belong to him; the sea, which
he made, is his along with
the dry ground, which his
own hands formed.

Psalm 95:4-5

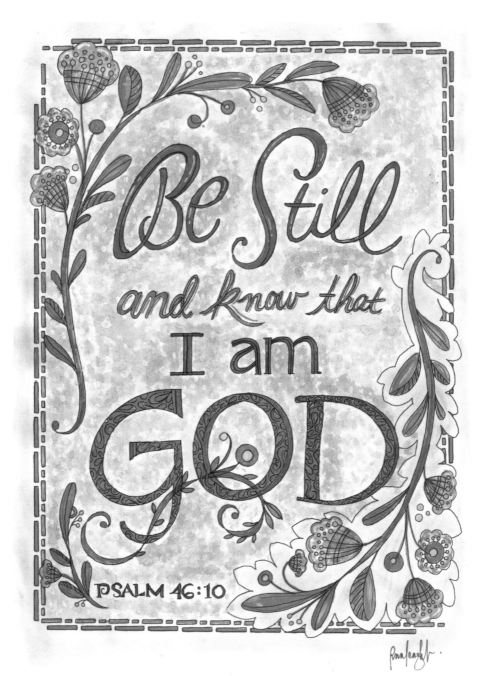

Do you think it's possible to experience God in other people, or with other people? Describe a time you felt God's presence in others—perhaps during worship, perhaps in another gathering, or perhaps simply in a crowd.

Before the mountains
were born, before you
birthed the earth and
the inhabited world—
from forever in the
past to forever in the
future, you are God.

Psalm 90:2

ABOUT THE ARTIST

Robin Pickens grew up in a creative family, making drawing and art a natural choice for her. After earning her BFA from the University of Michigan School of Art, Robin worked for many years as a successful broadcast television art director and animator. She then chose to pursue her passion for creating art that speaks from her heart and reflects her creative life as a wife and mother. Robin licenses her artwork for a variety of products, including Christmas ornaments, fabrics, calendars, greeting cards, gift books, home décor, wall art, dishware, and more. You can find more of Robin's work at *www.spoonflower.com/profiles/robinpickens* as well as through her website, *www.robinpickens.com*.

ISBN 978-1-64178-001-8

Fox Chapel Publishing makes every effort to use environmentally friendly paper for printing.

We are always looking for talented authors. To submit an idea, please send a brief inquiry to acquisitions@foxchapelpublishing.com.

Printed in China
First printing